D0768063

Published by Familius LLC, www.familius.com

Familius books are available at special discounts for bulk purchases for sales promotions or for
family or corporate use. Special editions, including personalized covers, excerpts of existing
books, or books with corporate logos, can be created in large quantities for special needs.
For more information, contact Premium Sales at 559-876-2170 or email
specialmarkets@familius.com.

Library of Congress Catalog-in-Publication Data

2015935371
pISBN 978-1-939629-68-5
eISBN 978-1-942672-12-8

Cover and book design by David Miles
Edited by Liza Hagerman

10 9 8 7 6 5 4 3 2 1

First Edition

Printed in China

QUINOA CRAZY

the GLUTEN-FREE SUPER FOOD COOKBOOK

BRITNEY RULE & CHERIE SCHETSELAAR

FAMILIUS

AUTHOR'S NOTE

....

My name is Britney, and Cherie is my mom. Food is intuitive for my mom. She can make bread or muffins without consulting a recipe. When she started changing recipes on her own to make them healthier, there was a problem. No one could replicate what she was making. Sometimes she couldn't even replicate what she had made to her satisfaction.

So I encouraged her to start a blog, and I promised to help her. This journey evolved into our first book, *Grain Crazy*, and then into this one—all about the wonderful "grain" superfood quinoa. We're not only crazy about quinoa, but we're also crazy about helping people eat healthier. We hope the recipes in this book provide an easy, healthful way to incorporate this beautiful food into your diet.

—*Britney Rule*

CONTENTS

QUINOA 101

WHAT'S THE BIG DEAL?

You've no doubt heard about quinoa. You've seen it in the health food aisle and tried to remember how, exactly, to say its name. (It's pronounced KEEN-wah, by the way.) Maybe you've even tried it out with varied results. But there must be a reason why it's so popular, right?

Well, there is. Actually, there are several reasons. Here are the three big ones:

1 It's a superfood, meaning that it's unusually nutritionally dense. Quinoa contains a large percentage of protein—at 12–18 percent, it's incredibly protein rich. It's also high in fiber, which aids in digestion, and is rich in minerals, including phosphorous, magnesium, manganese, iron, folate, copper, and calcium—all of which have a wide variety of health benefits. In addition to supplying such minerals, quinoa has been shown to contain antioxidant and anti-inflammatory phytonutrients (natural chemicals) that, though not essential to life, are beneficial.

2 It's gluten-free! Quinoa is not a grain; it is a seed more closely related to beetroots and spinach. However, it can be used in the same ways grain is used. This is incredibly helpful for the growing number of people with gluten sensitivities. It's also a big positive for those who are just looking to cut back on gluten in their diet, due to gluten overload. To capitalize on this, we've made all of the recipes in this book gluten-free. We don't recommend that everyone completely cut gluten from their diet, but since gluten is added to so many foods, it may still be beneficial for many people to cut down on the amount of gluten they eat.

3 Quinoa is a complete protein, which means that it contains all nine amino acids essential to life, making it a complete substitute for meat. It's great for vegetarians, vegans, or anyone looking to cut back on their meat intake. The majority of recipes in this book are meat-free.

Plus, it's delicious!

White Quinoa

Red Quinoa

BEFORE THE RECENT FAD

Is quinoa new? What makes it so popular with health foodies today? Where does it come from?

Quinoa is not a new food. It was a staple in pre-Colombian Incan culture. It was such an integral part of Incan life that it was known as "the mother of all grains" and was frequently used in religious ceremonies. When the Spanish conquistadors conquered the Incans, they forbade growing quinoa in an effort to squash the native religion in favor of Christianity, and they forced the Incans to grow wheat instead. Most of the world's quinoa is still grown high in the Peruvian Andes, where it was domesticated, though it's also being cultivated in parts of the United States, such as Colorado and Oregon.

There are reportedly over 1,800 varieties of quinoa, but only three are commonly sold in the United States: **white**, **red**, and **black**. You can also find tricolor mixtures. All quinoa essentially cooks the same and has similar nutrient content, but some people find red and black quinoa to have a slightly stronger flavor and be a little chewier than the white variety. We prefer to use white quinoa in place of flour or as a pilaf, and black or red quinoa in salads, but they are so similar that they are interchangeable.

Black Quinoa

HOW DO I USE QUINOA?

Quinoa can be used in any way you would use other grains. It cooks just as easily as rice or can be made into flour. Here are some of our favorite uses for it:

USE IT AS A NUTRIENT-DENSE RICE SUBSTITUTE

This is by far the easiest way to incorporate quinoa into your diet. Instead of having a bowl of white rice, lacking in vitamins and nutrients, enjoy a bowl of quinoa. Cook it just like rice in water or your choice of chicken or vegetable broth. Add other grains such as barley, buckwheat, or brown rice to vary your nutrient intake even more.

USE IT RAW

Quinoa adds a nice crunch to snacks and granolas.

USE IT AS A BREAKFAST CEREAL

Add cooked quinoa to your bowl of oatmeal, or just eat quinoa instead. It can be combined with many other grains besides oats, such as amaranth, buckwheat, or teff, to make a delicious start to your day. We like quinoa toasted to enhance its nutty flavor.

MAKE IT INTO FLOUR

Since quinoa doesn't contain gluten, it can't be easily used in breads that must rise. However, it can be used as flour in quick breads and desserts. The product will be denser than that of white flour—with a more truffle-like consistency.

ADD IT TO A SOUP

Grains are often added to soups with delicious results, and quinoa is no exception. Not only does quinoa add nutrients, but it also can turn a vegetarian soup into a complete protein.

PREPARING QUINOA

RINSING

Quinoa is covered in saponin (SAP-uh-nin), a bitter chemical that must be removed from quinoa before it can be eaten. Saponin naturally makes quinoa pest-free and easier to grow without pesticides, since birds and other animals are repelled by the taste. In South America, saponin is used as detergent for clothing and an antiseptic for skin injuries. Most quinoa packages at the store will be labeled "prewashed," but we find it helpful to rinse it again, just in case.

To remove the saponin, pour about 1 cup of quinoa into a 2-cup glass measuring cup, and then fill the remainder of the cup with water. If you stir it around, you will find the water becoming cloudy with saponin. Next, pour the water and quinoa into a fine wire strainer. Repeat until the water is mostly clear.

TOASTING

Toasting quinoa gives it a nutty, mild flavor. There are two ways to toast your quinoa: on the stove or in the oven.

To toast it on your stovetop, after rinsing well, place a saucepan on the stove at medium heat. Heat the quinoa, stirring frequently. Let it cook until it's a light golden color.

To toast it in the oven, after rinsing well, preheat your oven to 350 degrees, and put the quinoa on a cookie sheet. Bake for 10–15 minutes to dry it out and toast it. Remove the quinoa from the oven when it starts to turn golden brown.

Once your quinoa is toasted, you may cook it as you wish.

COOKING

You can cook quinoa that has been toasted or is raw. We usually use water, chicken broth, or vegetable broth for our liquid.

For every 1 cup of quinoa, bring 2 cups of liquid to a boil in a pot. Add the rinsed quinoa and any desired spices to the liquid and turn the heat down to low. Cover and let it cook for 15–20 minutes or until all water has been absorbed. When the quinoa is properly done, you will see little tails emerging from the seeds. At this point, remove the quinoa from heat and use it hot or cold.

If you generally cook rice in a rice or pressure cooker, quinoa can also be cooked in these appliances. Follow the manufacturer's instructions for cooking whole grains.

GRINDING INTO FLOUR

Rinse the quinoa well, and toast it either on the stove or in the oven. When cool, run the quinoa through your grain grinder. If you don't have a grain grinder, you can also grind quinoa in a coffee grinder, although the texture might not be as fine as that of the flour you'd find in the store.

Disclaimer: Many of the recipes in this book call for old-fashioned oats, which are naturally gluten-free. However, such oats often contain trace amounts of gluten, since they are usually processed with wheat and cross-contamination may occur. If you have gluten sensitivities, please take caution and only use oats that are certified gluten-free.

When cooking quinoa, use 2 parts liquid for every 1 part quinoa.

BREAK FAST

BASIC TOASTED QUINOA CEREAL

WE LOVE EATING QUINOA AS CEREAL FOR BREAKFAST. FULL OF PROTEIN AND FIBER, IT LEAVES US FEELING SATISFIED AND KEEPS OUR BELLIES FULL UNTIL LUNCH. IT SEEMS TO GIVE US AN ENERGY BOOST IN THE MORNING, TOO.

INGREDIENTS

1/2 cup quinoa, uncooked and well rinsed

1 tablespoon coconut oil

1 cup almond milk, unsweetened

1/2 cup water

1 tablespoon honey or another sweetener of your choice

1/2 teaspoon cinnamon

Fresh cherries, chopped, or your favorite fruit for topping (optional)

Extra milk (optional)

SERVES 2

1 Heat a small saucepan on medium heat.

2 Pour in the quinoa and oil and cook, stirring frequently, until the quinoa is a light golden color.

3 Pour in the milk, water, honey, and cinnamon.

4 Let the mixture come to a low boil. Turn down the heat to low and cook for about 20 minutes or until the liquid is absorbed.

5 Spoon the cereal into bowls and serve with cherries or your favorite fruit topping. Pour on a little more milk, if desired. Store leftovers in an airtight container in the refrigerator.

DID YOU KNOW?

The curly "tail" you see on a grain of quinoa is the germ of the seed—one of the most nutrient-dense parts of a grain. It usually separates slightly from the rest of the grain just as quinoa finishes cooking.

QUINOA BUCKWHEAT OATMEAL HOT CEREAL

BUCKWHEAT IS NEITHER A GRAIN NOR A TYPE OF WHEAT; IT'S A FRUIT SEED THAT CAN BE USED AS A GRAIN, AND WE LOVE THAT IT'S GLUTEN-FREE. BUCKWHEAT AND QUINOA MAKE A FANTASTIC PAIRING WITH OATS IN THIS RECIPE.

1 In a medium saucepan, toast the quinoa for a few minutes on medium heat, stirring frequently, until it turns a light golden color.

2 Add the buckwheat, oats, water, milk, honey, and oil. Let the mixture come to a boil and cook 2–3 minutes. Turn the heat down to low and cover. Let the mixture cook for about 20 minutes, stirring occasionally. Add additional water if needed.

3 When the oatmeal gets to your desired consistency, remove from heat and scoop into bowls. I like to leave some texture in my oatmeal.

4 Sprinkle on the spices, chopped fruit, and extra milk (if desired). Leftovers can be stored in a covered container in the refrigerator for a couple of days.

INGREDIENTS

1 cup quinoa, uncooked and well rinsed

1/2 cup buckwheat, uncooked

1/2 cup old-fashioned oats

2 cups water

1 cup vanilla almond milk, unsweetened

2 tablespoons honey

1 tablespoon coconut oil

Nutmeg and cinnamon to taste

Your favorite fruit, chopped for topping (optional)

Almond milk, unsweetened (optional)

SERVES 4

TIP:
We like to grate whole nutmeg and cinnamon sticks. It makes the spices taste fresher.

QUINOA OATMEAL
WITH STRAWBERRIES AND BANANAS

QUINOA IS A GREAT CHOICE FOR BREAKFAST BECAUSE IT STARTS OFF YOUR DAY WITH A HEFTY SOURCE OF PROTEIN. WE ADD FRUIT TOPPINGS FOR NATURAL SWEETNESS AND A BIT OF CHIA FOR A SUPPLEMENTAL NUTRITIONAL BOOST.

INGREDIENTS

1/3 cup quinoa, uncooked and well rinsed

1/3 cup old-fashioned oats

2 tablespoons chia seeds

1/2 cup water

1 cup vanilla almond milk, unsweetened

1 tablespoon honey

1 tablespoon coconut oil

Strawberries and bananas, chopped, for topping

Almond milk, unsweetened (optional)

SERVES 2

1 In a medium saucepan, toast the quinoa for a few minutes on medium heat, stirring frequently until it turns a light golden color.

2 Stir in the oats, chia, water, milk, honey, and oil. Bring to a boil and cook for 1–2 minutes.

3 Turn down the heat to medium-low and cover. Stir the oatmeal occasionally until thickened. Add additional water if needed.

4 Remove from heat and serve the oatmeal in bowls.

5 Top with fruit. Drizzle milk on top if desired.

DID YOU KNOW?

Chia seeds are a powerhouse of omega-3 fatty acids, magnesium, iron, calcium, potassium, and vitamin C. Chia aids weight loss because it expands in your belly and naturally gives you the sensation of being full. It also has more antioxidants per serving than any other whole food, including blueberries.

QUINOA SMOOTHIE

WE LIKE TO ADD QUINOA TO SMOOTHIES FOR A BOOST OF PROTEIN. THINK OF IT AS AN
INCREDIBLE, NATURAL PROTEIN POWDER!

INGREDIENTS

1 cup almond milk, unsweetened

1 cup peaches, frozen

2 bananas, frozen

1/2 cup quinoa, uncooked and well rinsed

1 teaspoon vanilla

SERVES 2

1 Mix all ingredients in a blender until smooth.

2 Serve immediately.

OATMEAL TEFF QUINOA PANCAKES

THESE PANCAKES ARE DELIGHTFUL, USING THREE DELICIOUS WHOLE GRAINS WITH DISTINCT HEALTH BENEFITS: OATS, TEFF, AND QUINOA. WE LOVE THESE GRAINS AND THIS RECIPE'S CINNAMON-ORANGE FLAVOR.

1 Blend dry ingredients together in a large bowl.

2 In another bowl, mix all the wet ingredients together.

3 Add the wet ingredients to the dry ingredients. Mix all until just blended—but don't overmix.

4 On a hot skillet, pour batter into 4-inch pancakes. Cook on both sides until golden brown.

5 Serve with your favorite sweet topping.

SERVES 4

TIP:

We love to use different grains in our cooking in addition to quinoa. Each grain contains different vitamins and minerals to add to a balanced diet. Teff, for example, is gluten-free, high in protein and fiber, and supplies more calcium than milk. Many stores are starting to carry flours made from these grains, but if you can't find them at your local grocery store, try the health foods store or buy the grains and grind your own.

INGREDIENTS

2 1/2 cups oat flour

1/2 cup teff flour

1/4 cup quinoa flour

1 teaspoon baking powder

1/2 teaspoon baking soda

1/2 teaspoon salt

1 teaspoon cinnamon

1/3 cup honey

2 1/2 cups buttermilk

2 large eggs

1/4 cup orange juice

1 teaspoon vanilla

2 teaspoons orange zest

2 tablespoons coconut oil

Toppings (apple pie filling, jam, or buttermilk syrup)

SPROUTED QUINOA MILK

DID YOU KNOW THAT YOU CAN MAKE QUINOA MILK? WE WERE FASCINATED TO FIND THAT OUT. IT IS ANOTHER GREAT NON-DAIRY CHOICE. YOU CAN DECIDE WHAT SPICES YOU WANT TO ADD TO IT, BUT THE SPICES LISTED HERE CREATE A CHAI-LIKE FLAVOR. IT IS A CREAMY TREAT TO POUR OVER HOT CEREAL.

INGREDIENTS

1/2 cup quinoa, uncooked and well rinsed

2 cups water

1 tablespoon honey

1/2 teaspoon vanilla

1/2 teaspoon cinnamon

1/8 teaspoon allspice

1/8 teaspoon cloves, ground

1/4 teaspoon nutmeg

1/4 teaspoon cardamom

SERVES 2

1 In a small mesh strainer, rinse the quinoa off several times. Then pour it into a bowl covered with water and let it soak for 3–4 hours.

2 Drain the quinoa in the mesh strainer again. Let it sit for 8–10 hours in the strainer over a bowl, covered with a towel, to let it sprout.

3 Pour the sprouted grains into a blender with water, honey, vanilla, and spices. Blend all the ingredients until completely smooth.

4 Use the quinoa milk in place of regular milk. Store it in the refrigerator for up to 2 days. Shake or stir before drinking if settling occurs.

TIP:

Letting the quinoa sprout makes it a little sweeter, makes it easier to digest, and gives it greater nutritional value.

QUINOA, AMARANTH, AND BUCKWHEAT HOT CEREAL

"SOME LIKE IT HOT, SOME LIKE IT COLD . . . " WE LOVE THIS CEREAL, AND IT IS DELICIOUS HOT OR COLD. THE TEXTURE IS SIMILAR TO THAT OF RICE PUDDING.

1 Boil the water, then stir in all the ingredients except the raisins or dried fruit and the optional extra almond milk.

2 Turn the heat down to low, cover, and cook until all the grains are softened, about 10 minutes. Add more water if needed.

3 Add raisins or dried fruit and top with extra almond milk, if desired. Serve at your preferred temperature. Store the leftovers in an airtight container in the refrigerator.

DID YOU KNOW?

You may be wondering: *What is amaranth?* Amaranth seeds come from many species of amaranthus plants, which are known for their colorful flowers. True to the Greek word, *amarantos*—meaning "unfading"—the flowers don't wither or fade, even after being harvested. Similar to quinoa, amaranth is a protein powerhouse, low in cholesterol, and gluten-free!

INGREDIENTS

3 cups water

1/3 cup almond milk, unsweetened

1/3 cup quinoa, uncooked and well rinsed

1/3 cup buckwheat, uncooked

1/3 cup amaranth, uncooked

1/3 cup coconut oil

1 teaspoon cinnamon

2–3 tablespoons honey

1/4 teaspoon nutmeg

1/3 cup raisins, dried cranberries, dates, or other dried fruit (optional)

Extra almond milk, unsweetened (optional)

SERVES 4

BERRY YOGURT BOWL

THIS BERRY BOWL IS LIKE A PARFAIT WITHOUT ALL THE WORK—A TREAT THAT HELPS US GET OUT OF THE RUT OF CEREAL. THE COLLECTION OF PROTEIN-FILLED YOGURT, NUTS, SEEDS, AND FRUIT IS A POWERHOUSE OF VITAMINS AND MINERALS THAT STARTS YOUR DAY OFF RIGHT.

INGREDIENTS

1 cup plain Greek yogurt

1 tablespoon honey

2 tablespoons raw, unsalted cashews, chopped

2 tablespoons almonds, chopped

2 tablespoons quinoa, uncooked and well rinsed

2 tablespoons chia seeds

1/4 cup berries or bananas

SERVES 1

1 Mix together the yogurt and honey.

2 Place the yogurt in a serving dish. Top with cashews, almonds, quinoa, chia, and berries or bananas.

3 Serve immediately.

QUINOA WAFFLES

WAFFLES ARE ONE OF MY KIDS' FAVORITE FOODS, ESPECIALLY FOR DINNER. THESE CRISPY, GOLDEN CLASSICS ARE GREAT ANYTIME.

INGREDIENTS

2 cups quinoa flour

2 tablespoons cornmeal

3 tablespoons cornstarch

1 teaspoon salt

1/2 teaspoon baking soda

2 large eggs

1/4 cup coconut oil, melted

1 3/4 cups kefir or buttermilk

3 tablespoons honey

Fresh fruit, chopped for topping (optional)

MAKES 8 WAFFLES

1 In a medium bowl, mix the flour, cornmeal, cornstarch, salt, and baking soda with a wire whisk. Set aside.

2 In a separate bowl, mix the eggs, oil, kefir, and honey. Stir the wet ingredients into the flour mixture until flour is moistened.

3 Set the batter aside for 5–10 minutes. This lets it expand and makes for lighter waffles and pancakes.

4 Bake the waffles in a preheated waffle iron. Serve while warm with fresh fruit, if desired.

TIP:

Have you ever used kefir before? It is similar to yogurt in that it is a powerhouse of bacteria that are healthy for your gut, such as acidophilus.

CHILE RELLENO QUICHES

CHILIES, CHEESE, AND GREEN ONIONS PAIR PERFECTLY WITH EGGS AND QUINOA IN THIS SAVORY DISH. WE PULL THE QUICHES BUBBLING FROM THE OVEN AND SERVE THEM WHEN JUST COOL ENOUGH TO EAT.

1 Preheat oven to 400 degrees.

2 Distribute the first four ingredients equally in four 4-inch ramekins.

3 In a small bowl, beat together the eggs, skim milk, and salt. Pour the mixture into the ramekins in equal portions.

4 Put the dishes on a cookie sheet and place the entire cookie sheet in oven. Cook for 20 minutes. Let cool and then serve.

INGREDIENTS

1 can (4 ounces) diced green chilies

1/2 cup quinoa, cooked

2 green onions

1/2 cup jack cheese, grated

3 egg whites

1 egg

3/4 cup skim milk

Dash of salt

MAKES 4 QUICHES

QUINOA AND EGGS MEXICAN STYLE

WE LIKE TO MAKE THIS MEAL DURING THE SUMMER BECAUSE IT DOESN'T HEAT UP THE KITCHEN. IT CAN BE SERVED ANY TIME OF DAY.

1 In a medium saucepan, toast the quinoa for a few minutes on medium heat, stirring frequently, until it turns a light golden color. In a large saucepan, boil the water. Stir in the quinoa and turn down the heat. Put on the lid and let the water absorb, stirring occasionally.

2 In a bowl, beat the eggs, salt, pepper, garlic powder, and milk together.

3 Heat a skillet to medium heat. Melt the butter in the pan. Then pour in the egg mixture. Let cook about 3 minutes, stirring as needed to cook thoroughly.

4 Turn the heat down to medium-low. Add the mushrooms, tomatoes, onions, chilies, and cooked quinoa. Add 1/4 cup water if there is not enough liquid. Stir the mixture, cover, and cook for a few minutes.

INGREDIENTS

1/2 cup quinoa, uncooked and well rinsed

1 1/2 cups water

7 eggs

1 teaspoon salt

1/2 teaspoon freshly ground pepper

1/2 teaspoon garlic powder

1/2 cup milk

1 tablespoon butter

1 can (4 ounces) chopped mushrooms, drained

1 can (15 ounces) diced tomatoes, drained

4 green onions, chopped

1 can (4 ounces) diced green chilies

1/2 cup cheese, grated

Cilantro for garnish

Salsa

SERVES 4

5 When the mixture has thickened, mix some cilantro in, if desired, and add the cheese. Cover long enough for the cheese to melt. Garnish with cilantro. Serve with salsa.

BERRIES AND CREAM
WITH QUINOA PORRIDGE

SOME PEOPLE THINK IT'S YUMMY TO POUR CREAM OVER BERRIES WITHOUT EVEN WHIPPING IT. MOM DECIDED TO MAKE A HEALTHIER VERSION BY USING COCONUT MILK, WITH ADDED QUINOA FOR EXTRA NUTRITION. WE ENJOYED IT FOR BREAKFAST.

1 In a medium saucepan, toast the quinoa for a few minutes on medium heat, stirring frequently, until it turns a light golden color.

2 Stir in the chia (if desired), milk, water, honey, and oil. Let the mixture come to a low boil for a couple of minutes, stirring a few times as it cooks.

3 Turn the heat down to low and cover, stirring occasionally. Cook for 20–30 minutes or until completely softened.

4 Pour the porridge into individual bowls and top with coconut milk and berries.

INGREDIENTS

1 cup quinoa, uncooked and well rinsed

3 tablespoons chia seeds (optional)

1 cup milk of your choosing

1 cup water

1 1/2 tablespoons honey

1 tablespoon coconut oil

Coconut milk

Mixed berries

SERVES 4

DID YOU KNOW?

How is porridge distinctive from soup? It is a dish created by boiling crushed or chopped grains in milk, water, or both until it has a thick consistency. It can be served sweet with fruit or savory with spices and vegetables.

SIDES

BASIC BROWN RICE AND QUINOA MIX

WE LOVE THIS SIMPLE SUBSTITUTE FOR PLAIN WHITE RICE—IT'S A GREAT STARTING POINT FOR MANY OTHER SIDES. BROWN RICE IS HIGH IN FIBER, HELPS LOWER CHOLESTEROL, AND CAN HELP REGULATE THYROID AND IMMUNE SYSTEM FUNCTIONS. IT PAIRS WONDERFULLY WITH QUINOA AS A SIDE DISH.

INGREDIENTS

1 cup brown rice, uncooked

1/2 cup quinoa, uncooked and well rinsed

3 cups water

Spices of your choice (we like marjoram, basil, or cilantro)

SERVES 6

1 Combine the ingredients in a pressure cooker, rice cooker, or on the stovetop, and cook like ordinary rice. The dish is done when soft and tender.

DID YOU KNOW?

Quinoa grows on large stalks 3 to 9 feet tall. The top of the stalk, which contains the seeds, can be red, green, purple, black, yellow, or pink. In addition to the grains, the quinoa plant's leaves are also edible and can be used as you would any other salad greens.

SHRIMP MANGO SALSA

WE LOVE SHRIMP, AND THIS DELICIOUS, DECADENT APPETIZER IS SURE TO IMPRESS YOUR FAMILY AND FRIENDS.

1 Chop the shrimp into bite-sized pieces and place them in a large bowl.

2 Add the remaining ingredients to the bowl of shrimp. Toss the mixture together.

INGREDIENTS

1 pound medium shrimp, cooked, unshelled, deveined, and de-tailed

Vegetable oil or cooking spray

1 cup quinoa, cooked

1/4 cup cilantro, chopped

1 tablespoon olive oil

1/2 teaspoon salt

1 large mango, peeled and diced

1/2 avocado, peeled and diced

1 medium tomato, diced

1/8 red onion, finely chopped

1 serrano pepper, deseeded and finely diced

1 tablespoon fresh lime juice

Salt and pepper to taste

SERVES 8

ASPARAGUS EGG SKILLET

WE LOVE FINDING NEW WAYS TO EAT VEGETABLES. IT IS EASY TO GET IN A RUT AND EAT THE SAME ONES ALL THE TIME. ASPARAGUS IS A GREAT VEGETABLE WITH LOTS OF HEALTH BENEFITS. THE MOST IMPORTANT THING TO REMEMBER WITH ASPARAGUS IS TO NOT OVERCOOK IT. LET IT KEEP ITS PRETTY BRIGHT GREEN COLOR.

INGREDIENTS

2 tablespoons olive oil

1 clove garlic

1 onion, sliced

9 asparagus spears, cut into 2-inch slices

3 eggs

1 cup red quinoa, cooked

Salt and pepper to taste

Fresh marjoram (optional)

1 tomato, diced

SERVES 6

1 In a large saucepan, heat the oil, garlic, and onion for 2–3 minutes on medium-high heat. Add asparagus. Cook until just soft.

2 Remove 2 asparagus spears from the pan and chop them into bite-sized pieces. Set them aside.

3 Add the eggs to the remaining asparagus and cook thoroughly.

4 Add the quinoa, salt, and pepper. Stir together gently, and heat until just warm. Add marjoram on top for garnish, if desired.

5 Top dish with reserved asparagus and diced tomato.

TIP:
To keep asparagus fresh longer, store stalks in a tall container with one inch of water in the bottom and a bag over the top.

ITALIAN BITES

MOM RAVED ABOUT THESE ITALIAN BITES FOR DAYS. SHE IS SURE YOU WILL ENJOY THEM TOO.

INGREDIENTS

1 cup quinoa, cooked

1 egg

1/4 teaspoon dried rosemary

1 teaspoon salt

2 tablespoons olive oil

1/4 teaspoon oregano

1/4 teaspoon garlic powder

1/4 teaspoon basil

MAKES 8 BITES

1 Measure all ingredients into a bowl. Stir until combined.

2 Place the mixture in the refrigerator for 15–30 minutes to harden.

3 Take the solidified mixture out of the refrigerator. Preheat the oven to 350 degrees.

4 Press the mixture into 1-inch balls and place the balls on a cookie sheet. If you have a small cookie scoop, that will work best. Just scoop the mixture, pressing it against the inside of the bowl to keep the ball together.

5 Place the bites in the hot oven. Cook for 8–10 minutes.

6 Take out the bites and serve warm. Store the leftovers in an airtight container in the refrigerator.

LIME QUINOA

THIS IS A SIMPLE DISH WITH JUST A BIT OF SPICE. WE ENJOY IT AS A SIDE WITH MEXICAN FOOD OR GRILLED CHICKEN.

1 In a big bowl, toss all the ingredients together. Be careful not to overmix as the quinoa could become mushy.

TIP:
Next time you're cooking quinoa, make a big batch and freeze it so it is ready to go for recipes like this one. It saves on prep time and encourages you to use whole grains more frequently.

INGREDIENTS

2 cups quinoa, cooked

1/3 cup cilantro, chopped

2 tablespoons fresh lime juice

1/2 teaspoon lime zest

Salt and pepper to taste

SERVES 8

QUINOA HUMMUS

THIS SIMPLE HUMMUS IS EVEN MORE FLAVORFUL DUE TO THE ADDITION OF QUINOA.
SERVE WITH GLUTEN-FREE PITA, CORN CHIPS, OR FRESH VEGETABLE STICKS. WE ALSO
ENJOY ADDING IT TO A FAVORITE WRAP OR SANDWICH AS A HEALTHY SPREAD.

1 Pour all ingredients into a food processor or blender.

2 Blend until the mixture is smooth and creamy.

INGREDIENTS

1 can (15.5 ounces) chickpeas, rinsed and drained

1 cup quinoa, cooked

2 1/2 tablespoons olive oil

2 1/2 tablespoons water

1/2 clove garlic

1/2 teaspoon salt

SERVES 8

DID YOU KNOW?

Chickpeas are also known as "garbanzo beans." Look for them with the canned beans in your grocery store.

SPANISH QUINOA

THE NEXT TIME YOU FEEL TEMPTED TO MAKE SPANISH RICE, MAKE SPANISH QUINOA INSTEAD. IN PLACE OF A BOWL FULL OF CARBS, YOU'LL HAVE A FILLING BOWL OF NUTRIENTS, INCLUDING MAGNESIUM, IRON, CALCIUM, AND FIBER.

INGREDIENTS

2 tablespoons olive oil

1/2 green pepper, chopped

1/3 onion, chopped

1/2 jalapeño, deseeded and minced

1/4 teaspoon chili powder

2 cloves garlic, minced

1/2 teaspoon cumin

Salt and pepper to taste

3 Roma tomatoes

1 cup quinoa, cooked

SERVES 4

1 Warm skillet on medium heat. Heat up the olive oil.

2 Stir in everything except the tomatoes and quinoa. Let the vegetables sauté as you stir them, about 5 minutes, or until softened.

3 Add the tomatoes and let the mixture cook another couple of minutes to let the flavors meld together. Toss in the cooked quinoa and cook another couple of minutes, being careful to not overstir.

4 Remove from heat when warmed all the way through. Serve immediately.

RED QUINOA AND ZUCCHINI

ZUCCHINI IS ONE OF THE EASIEST THINGS TO GROW IN THE ROCKY MOUNTAIN AREA WHERE WE LIVE—SO MUCH SO THAT WE OFTEN STRUGGLE TO USE IT ALL! THIS SIDE DISH IS A WONDERFUL WAY TO INCORPORATE ZUCCHINI INTO OUR DIETS.

1 In a large skillet, warm olive oil on medium heat. Add zucchini and sauté until it begins to soften.

2 Add the red quinoa and heat until warmed through. Toss in the thyme and garlic. Add salt and pepper to taste.

3 Remove from heat and serve while warm.

INGREDIENTS

1 1/2 tablespoons olive oil

2 cups zucchini, thinly sliced

1 cup red quinoa, cooked

1/2 teaspoon thyme

2 cloves garlic, minced

Salt and pepper to taste

SERVES 6

DID YOU KNOW?

Zucchini is actually a fruit, though it is normally cooked as if it were a vegetable. Zucchini is naturally low in calories yet high in folate, vitamin A, and potassium.

MEXICAN QUINOA

THIS DISH ISN'T A VARIATION OF THE RICE THAT YOU'D GET AT A MEXICAN RESTAURANT. WE FIND IT IS A MUCH FRESHER ALTERNATIVE AND A WONDERFUL SIDE TO ANY MEAL.

INGREDIENTS

2/3 cup white quinoa, uncooked and well rinsed

1 1/3 cups water

1 1/2 teaspoons red pepper flakes

2 teaspoons paprika

1/2 teaspoon chili powder

1 teaspoon salt

1/2 teaspoon pepper

1 can (15 ounces) black beans, drained and rinsed

2 tomatoes, chopped

1 red pepper, chopped

1/2 cup cilantro, chopped

SERVES 8

1 Pour quinoa into a medium saucepan with water, red pepper, paprika, chili powder, salt, and pepper. Bring to a boil, and then reduce heat to a simmer.

2 Cover and continue to simmer the mixture for about 15 minutes or until all water has evaporated. Remove from heat.

3 Place the quinoa in a large bowl and toss in the beans, tomatoes, and peppers. Top with cilantro.

DID YOU KNOW?

Quinoa may help lower the risk of diabetes. It is low on the glycemic index, meaning it won't cause a spike in blood sugar. Quinoa also contains magnesium, which promotes healthy blood sugar levels.

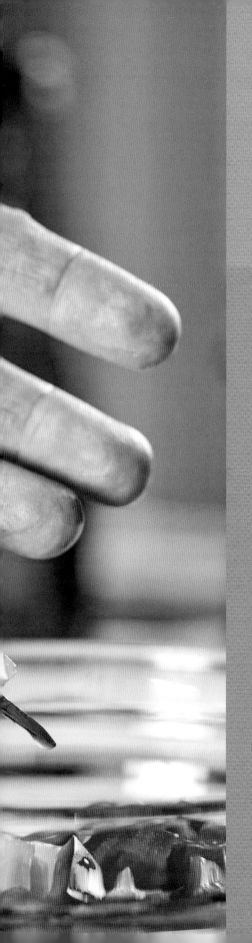

SALADS

RED QUINOA VEGGIE SALAD WITH AVOCADO DRESSING

THIS TEMPTING SALAD WITH FRESH AVOCADOS IN THE DRESSING IS AN APPETIZING WAY FOR US TO EAT MORE VEGETABLES.

1 Toss the salad ingredients together in a large bowl.

2 Pour all the dressing ingredients into a blender and pulse until creamy. It may take a little stirring in between pulsing to mix completely.

3 Store the dressing and salad separately in the refrigerator, covered, until ready to serve.

SERVES 8

INGREDIENTS

SALAD

2 cups red or white quinoa, cooked

1/2 red pepper, deseeded and chopped

1/2 yellow pepper, deseeded and chopped

5 radishes, thinly sliced

1 cup zucchini, chopped

1/2 cup broccoli, chopped

1/4 cup purple onion, minced

DRESSING

2 ripe avocados, pitted

1/4 teaspoon salt

Juice from 1 lime

1/4 cup olive oil

2 tablespoons chili powder

1/4 cup plain yogurt

2 cloves garlic

APPLE GRAPE QUINOA SALAD

THIS FRUIT SALAD CONTAINS HONEYED NUTS AND A LIGHT OLIVE-OIL-AND-HONEY GLAZE. WE FIND THAT IT'S PERFECT IN THE SUMMER OR FALL.

INGREDIENTS

DRESSING

1/2 teaspoon salt

1 tablespoon olive oil

1/2 teaspoon lemon juice

1 tablespoon honey

SALAD

1 green apple, julienned (sliced into matchstick-sized or long, thin strips)

2 cups red grapes, sliced

1/4 cup dried cranberries

3/4 cup quinoa, cooked

1/4 cup chopped walnuts

1 tablespoon honey

SERVES 6

1 Mix together the salt, olive oil, lemon juice, and honey in a small bowl to make the dressing.

2 Place the sliced apples and grapes in a larger bowl. Toss with the dressing. Mix in the cranberries and quinoa.

3 Put the walnuts and honey in a small saucepan and cook on medium heat. Stir frequently, until the honey starts to thicken.

4 Serve the salad on individual plates. Top with honeyed walnuts.

DID YOU KNOW?

Grapes of all colors are not only tasty, they are good for you, too. Grapes contain resveratrol, an antioxidant that appears to be involved in reducing the risk or slowing the development of cancer, heart disease, degenerative nerve disease, viral infections, and Alzheimer's disease. Resveratrol is found particularly in the skins of grapes.

QUINOA FRUIT SALAD

WE THINK THIS SALAD IS A WONDERFUL WAY TO BRIGHTEN UP YOUR TABLE IN THE WINTER, WHEN POMEGRANATES SEEM TO FREQUENTLY GRACE THE SHELVES AT GROCERY STORES.

1 Put all the fruit in a bowl except for the pomegranate seeds.

2 Toss in the quinoa and lemon juice.

3 Toss in the pomegranate seeds last. Stir in yogurt, if desired. Serve as soon as possible.

TIP:

Do you love pomegranates but find it a huge pain to pull out all the little seeds and separate them from the pulp? Here's a quick way to change that:

1. Cut the pomegranate in half. Gently push on the skin to slightly loosen it from the pulp, without removing it.

2. Over a large bowl, place the pomegranate face down in your palm, fingers outspread. Using a wooden spoon, beat the outside of the pomegranate with several forceful blows. Most of the seeds should come out in your hand and fall into the bowl. Repeat as necessary to remove the remaining seeds.

3. Repeat the same process with the other half of the pomegranate. Pick out the few pulp pieces that come out as well. There should not be many.

INGREDIENTS

2 apples, chopped into bite-sized pieces

2 oranges, chopped into bite-sized pieces

1 cup grapes

1/2 cup quinoa, cooked

1 teaspoon lemon juice

1/2 cup pomegranate seeds

Plain yogurt (optional)

SERVES 4–6

TROPICAL BERRY SALAD

MOM AND I BOTH LOVE TO TRAVEL—ESPECIALLY TO TROPICAL LOCALES. BUT WHEN WE AREN'T ABLE TO MAKE IT THERE IN PERSON, SOMETIMES A TROPICAL FRUIT SALAD CAN MAKE HOME FEEL LIKE PARADISE.

INGREDIENTS

1/2 cup red quinoa, uncooked and well rinsed

1 cup fresh pineapple, diced

1/2 cup blueberries

1/2 cup mangoes, diced

1/2 cup blackberries

1/2 cup strawberries, diced

1 tablespoon honey

SERVES 6

1 Gently toss all ingredients together until honey is evenly distributed. Serve immediately.

SPINACH VEGGIE SALAD WITH CAESAR DRESSING

THIS LOW-CALORIE SALAD MAKES IT EASY FOR US TO ENJOY VEGETABLES WITH A DELICIOUS, SIMPLE DRESSING.

1 Evenly distribute the spinach in separate serving dishes, and toss in the different vegetables and quinoa.

2 Pour all the dressing ingredients in a blender. Mix for 2–3 minutes. Serve over spinach salad or let guests pour their own.

SERVES 2–4

INGREDIENTS

SALAD

1 avocado, diced

1 red bell pepper, diced

2 stalks green onion, diced

2 cups spinach

1 cup red quinoa, cooked

DRESSING

2 cloves garlic, minced

2 teaspoons spicy brown or Dijon mustard

2 teaspoons vinegar

1 tablespoon gluten-free mayonnaise

1/4 cup olive oil

Salt and pepper to taste (freshly ground pepper is wonderful)

1/2 teaspoon lemon juice

RADISH SALAD

THIS IS ONE OF THE SIMPLEST SALADS WE MAKE, BUT YOU'LL FIND YOU LOVE THE SIMPLE, PUNGENT CRUNCH OF VEGGIES THAT COMES THROUGH.

INGREDIENTS

4 radishes, diced

2 green onions, diced

1/2 cup snow peas

1/2 cup red quinoa, cooked

Seasoned rice vinegar

Salt and pepper to taste

1 Toss the vegetables, quinoa, and vinegar in a bowl, using just enough vinegar to slightly season the vegetables. Salt and pepper to taste.

SERVES 6

DID YOU KNOW?

Radishes are eaten all over the world. In Oaxaca, Mexico, people celebrate the "Night of the Radishes" as part of Christmas celebrations, in which giant radishes are carved into people, buildings, and other objects.

SNACKS

CHOCOLATE PEANUT BUTTER QUINOA GRANOLA

IT'S HARD TO GO WRONG WHEN YOU PUT PEANUT BUTTER AND CHOCOLATE TOGETHER. WHY NOT IN GRANOLA? WE ADD QUINOA FOR A LITTLE EXTRA CRUNCH IN THIS RECIPE.

INGREDIENTS

1/4 cup honey

1 tablespoon cocoa

1/2 cup natural peanut butter

2 tablespoons coconut oil

2 teaspoons vanilla

1/2 cup quinoa, well rinsed and toasted

1 1/2 cups old-fashioned oats

1/2 cup cashews or nuts of your choice, chopped

1/2 cup dark chocolate chips

SERVES 6

1 In a small saucepan on low heat, combine honey, cocoa, peanut butter, oil, and vanilla. Stir and let the mixture barely come to a boil. Remove from heat.

2 In a medium bowl, mix together quinoa and oats. Pour the warm chocolate mixture on top. Stir together until combined.

3 Spread across a cookie sheet.

4 Bake at 350 degrees until crunchy, about 15 minutes. Once cool, toss in the nuts and chips.

CHOCOLATE PEANUT BUTTER PROTEIN CANDY BITES

THESE NO-BAKE PROTEIN BITES TASTE LIKE A COMBINATION OF NESTLÉ® CRUNCH BARS AND PEANUT BUTTER CUPS.

INGREDIENTS

2 tablespoons cocoa

1 tablespoon honey

2 tablespoons coconut oil

1 teaspoon vanilla

1 cup natural peanut butter

1 cup quinoa, well rinsed and toasted

1/2 cup buckwheat groats, raw

1 Stir the cocoa, honey, coconut oil, vanilla, and peanut butter together in a bowl.

2 Add the quinoa and buckwheat and stir until all combined.

3 Scoop balls 1 inch to 1 1/2 inches in size, and put them on parchment paper on a cookie sheet. Place the cookie sheet in the refrigerator.

4 After the bites harden, enjoy or store them in the freezer until ready to eat.

MAKES 12 BITES

DID YOU KNOW?

In the culinary world, "groats" is a reference to any whole kernel of grain that has only undergone the minimal process of having its outer husk or hull removed. However, the word also refers to—as we do here—buckwheat in its whole kernel state.

BUCKWHEAT QUINOA POWER BITES

WE HAVE A WINNER! THESE SNACKS ARE A GREAT TREAT TO MAKE AHEAD OF TIME AND TAKE WITH YOU WHEN YOU NEED A HEALTHY SNACK. SUBSTITUTE THE CHOCOLATE CHIPS WITH 1/2 CUP DRIED FRUIT IF YOU'D LIKE THE BITES TO BE EVEN HEALTHIER.

1 Put all the ingredients in a blender or food processor. Pulse the blender until the mixture is combined. You will have to stop to scrape the blender and stir a couple times.

2 Scoop the batter into one-inch balls using your hands or a small cookie scoop. Add another 1/2 tablespoon coconut oil if they aren't sticking together well.

3 Eat the bites immediately or store them in an airtight container in the refrigerator. They will harden a little when cooled.

INGREDIENTS

3/4 cup buckwheat groats, raw

1/3 cup raw, unsalted cashews, chopped

1/2 cup quinoa, well rinsed and toasted

2 tablespoons honey

2 1/2 tablespoons coconut oil

1/3 cup dark chocolate chips

MAKES 8 BITES

DID YOU KNOW?

Many people think buckwheat is a cereal grain, but it's actually a fruit seed, meaning that, like quinoa, it's gluten-free! Even better, it is good for your cardiovascular system and lowers your risk of developing diabetes.

GRANOLA BITES

WE LOVE THESE YUMMY, PROTEIN-LOADED BARS. THEY WILL GIVE YOU A NATURAL ENERGY BOOST ANY TIME OF DAY. MAKE THEM AHEAD OF TIME AND STORE THEM IN AN AIRTIGHT CONTAINER IN THE REFRIGERATOR SO THAT YOU CAN HAVE THEM WHEN YOU WANT A GREAT SNACK.

1 Pour the almonds, sesame seeds, quinoa, oats, hemp, flaxseed, and chia into a medium bowl. Stir until completely blended.

2 Add water, honey, peanut butter, and coconut oil to the oat mixture. Fold in shredded coconut and chocolate chips. Mix until blended.

3 Firmly press the mixture into a 9x13-inch pan until level, using a spatula or plastic wrap. Allow it to sit in the refrigerator until firm.

4 Store the leftovers in an airtight container in the refrigerator.

INGREDIENTS

1 cup almonds, chopped

1/2 cup sesame seeds

1/2 cup quinoa, well rinsed and toasted

4 1/4 cups old-fashioned oats

1/4 cup Bob's Rod Mill® hemp seed

1/4 cup flaxseed, ground (optional)

1/4 cup chia seeds, ground (optional)

1/2 cup water

1/2 cup honey

1 1/2 cups natural peanut butter

2 tablespoons coconut oil

1/2 cup shredded coconut, unsweetened

1 cup dark chocolate chips

DID YOU KNOW?

Granola was invented in New York by Dr. James Caleb Jackson at the Jackson Sanitarium, a prominent health spa. The first granola (then called "granula") was made from graham flour and resembled an oversized version of Grape-Nuts® cereal.

SERVES 12

MULTIGRAIN PROTEIN BITES

WE ONLY NEED ONE OR TWO OF THESE BITES TO FEEL SATISFIED. THEY ARE A TASTY SNACK TO HAVE ON HAND FOR THOSE AFTERNOONS WHEN YOU NEED SOMETHING TO HOLD YOU OVER UNTIL DINNER.

INGREDIENTS

2 cups old-fashioned oats

1/2 cup quinoa, uncooked and well rinsed

1/2 cup shredded coconut, unsweetened

1/2 cup almond milk, unsweetened

1/4 cup chia seeds

4 tablespoons honey

3 tablespoons coconut oil

3 tablespoons peanut butter

1 teaspoon vanilla

1/2 cup dark chocolate chips, chopped

MAKES 24 BITES

1 Pour all ingredients into a large bowl except the chocolate chips, and stir until combined. Then stir in the chocolate chips.

2 Put the bowl in the refrigerator for at least 20 minutes to let the mixture harden.

3 Form the mixture into 1-inch balls using your hands or a small cookie scoop. Place the balls on parchment paper or wax paper on top of a cookie sheet.

4 Put the bites back in the refrigerator, and let them harden for about 30 minutes. Enjoy them, and store the leftovers in an airtight container in the refrigerator.

FROZEN CHOCOLATE BANANA BITES

IT HAS BEEN A LONG TIME SINCE I HAVE HAD A CHOCOLATE-COVERED BANANA. THESE LITTLE BITES BRING BACK FUN CHILDHOOD MEMORIES. THESE ARE ALSO YUMMY PROTEIN SNACKS THAT BOOST YOUR ENERGY.

1 In a medium bowl, blend together the bananas, quinoa, oats, and ground cashews or cashew butter.

2 Stir in the vanilla, honey, cinnamon, and oil. Put the mixture in the reezer or refrigerator for about 20 minutes to harden.

3 Take the bowl out and form the mixture into balls. Place in the freezer to harden for about 30 minutes.

4 In the meantime, melt the chocolate chips in a small bowl, and then stir in the oil. Place the chocolate in the refrigerator to thicken for 10 minutes.

5 Take the bites out of the freezer and the chocolate out of the refrigerator. Roll the bites in the chocolate and then in the nuts. Place on a greased cookie sheet.

6 Put the cookie sheet back into the freezer. Once the bites are frozen, enjoy them. Store leftovers in an airtight container in the freezer.

TIP:

To melt chocolate in the microwave, place the chips in a microwave-safe bowl. Turn down the power to 50 percent. Heat the chocolate chips for 30 seconds, then stir. Heat for another 20 seconds. Stir again. Heat again for 15 seconds and stir. Continue heating at decreasing intervals and stirring until the chocolate is melted. Do not overheat. Once the chocolate is melted, stop heating.

INGREDIENTS

2 ripe bananas, mashed

1 cup quinoa, cooked

1 cup old-fashioned oats

1/2 cup ground cashews or cashew butter

1 teaspoon vanilla

2 1/2 tablespoons honey

1 teaspoon cinnamon

1 1/2 tablespoons coconut oil

1/4 cup dark chocolate chips

1 tablespoon coconut oil

1/4 cup raw, unsalted cashews, chopped

MAKES 10 BITES

PROTEIN POWER BLAST TOPPING

THIS FUN TOPPING IS LOADED WITH PROTEIN. WE LIKE TO STORE IT IN AN AIRTIGHT CONTAINER IN THE REFRIGERATOR AND HAVE IT READY TO POUR ON TOP OF YOGURT, FRUIT, OR HOT CEREAL—OR EVEN EAT IT ALONE. THIS IS A GREAT WAY FOR YOU AND YOUR FAMILY AND FRIENDS TO ADD A PROTEIN BLAST TO YOUR DIET.

INGREDIENTS

1/2 cup peanut butter or your favorite nut butter

1/4 cup honey

1 1/2 cups old-fashioned oats

1 cup quinoa flour

1/2 cup shredded coconut, unsweetened

1/4 cup chia seeds

1/4 cup flaxseed, ground (optional)

1 teaspoon vanilla

1/2 cup dark chocolate chips, crushed

1/2 cup raisins or chopped nuts (optional)

1 In a large bowl, mix together the peanut butter and honey until creamy.

2 Pour in the oats, quinoa flour, coconut, chia, flaxseed, and vanilla. Blend until crumbly. We use our hands to get it all mixed together.

3 Stir in the chocolate chips and nuts or raisins, if desired.

4 Eat immediately or store in an airtight container in the refrigerator. Enjoy a yummy blast of flavor.

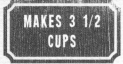

MAKES 3 1/2 CUPS

TIP:

Mix a couple tablespoons of topping with a couple tablespoons of nut butter. Stir together until combined. Spread on bread, crackers, fruit, or rice cakes.

QUINOA OAT BITES

WE LOVE ADDING QUINOA TO THESE PROTEIN BITES FOR MORE NUTRITION. THE RED QUINOA ADDS A COLORFUL FEATURE TO THE BITES AS WELL. THEY ARE GREAT PROTEIN SNACKS FOR ANY TIME OF THE DAY.

1 Pour the quinoa, oats, oil, honey, and cashew butter into a bowl and stir together until all ingredients are combined.

2 Fold in the chocolate chips and coconut.

3 Form the mixture into balls using a cookie scoop or your hands. Place on a lined cookie sheet. Put in the refrigerator to harden for about an hour.

4 Enjoy them, and store leftovers in an airtight container in the refrigerator.

INGREDIENTS

1 cup quinoa, cooked (red adds nice color)

1/2 cup old-fashioned oats

2 tablespoons coconut oil

3 tablespoons honey

4 tablespoons cashew butter

1/4 cup dark chocolate chips, ground

1/4 cup shredded coconut, unsweetened

MAKES 10 BITES

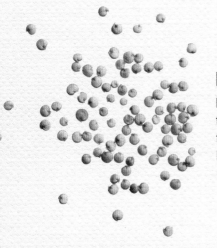

DID YOU KNOW?

NASA has studied quinoa and reported that it would be an ideal food source for long-term human space missions because of its "high protein value and unique amino acid composition."

PEANUT BUTTER BANANA BARS

MY BOYS WERE AT MOM'S HOUSE WHEN SHE FIRST MADE THESE GRANOLA BARS, AND THEY LOVED THEM. BESIDES BEING A GREAT SOURCE OF PROTEIN, THEY ARE FANTASTIC IN A SCHOOL LUNCH, AS AN AFTERNOON SNACK, OR EVEN AS AN ON-THE-GO BREAKFAST.

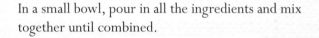

INGREDIENTS

1 ripe banana, mashed

1 3/4 cups old-fashioned oats

1/4 cup quinoa, uncooked and well rinsed

1/2 cup peanut butter or nut butter

1/2 teaspoon vanilla

1/4 cup honey

2 tablespoons coconut oil

SERVES 9

1 In a small bowl, pour in all the ingredients and mix together until combined.

2 Pour the mixture into a greased 9x9-inch pan and press down evenly. Cover the pan with plastic wrap.

3 Place the bars in the refrigerator for about an hour. Cut and serve when hardened.

4 Store leftovers in an airtight container in the refrigerator.

TRAIL MIX BALLS

WE LOVE THIS MEDLEY IN A YUMMY BITE. HIT THE TRAIL WITH THESE, OR JUST ENJOY THEM AS A GREAT SNACK. THEY ARE LOADED WITH PROTEIN, TOO, AS AN EXTRA BONUS.

1 Pour all the ingredients into a blender and pulse until the ingredients are broken down and well combined.

2 Form into 1-inch balls and place in an airtight container in the refrigerator until hardened.

3 Seve when hardened, and store leftovers in an airtight container in the refrigerator.

INGREDIENTS

1 cup old-fashioned oats

1/4 cup quinoa, uncooked and well rinsed

3/4 cup water

1/4 cup shredded coconut, unsweetened

1/3 cup sunflower seeds

1/2 cup dark chocolate chips

1/3 cup dried fruit

1 teaspoon vanilla

1/2 teaspoon salt

1 tablespoon peanut butter

1/3 cup honey

MAKES 12 BALLS

DID YOU KNOW?

Quinoa was an important food source for Incan warriors, who ate it for stamina on long marches and in battle.

BREADS

BANANA BLUEBERRY OATMEAL MUFFINS

THESE MUFFINS GET A BIG THUMBS-UP FROM THOSE WHO TRY THEM. MY SON JACOB WAS GOING FOR SECONDS AND THIRDS WHEN HE REMARKED, "THESE ARE DELICIOUS!" THAT IS A WINNER IN OUR BOOK.

INGREDIENTS

2 ripe bananas, mashed (about 1 cup)

3/4 cup plain yogurt

1/2 cup honey

2/3 cup coconut oil

4 teaspoons vanilla

2 cups quinoa flour

1 1/2 cups old-fashioned oats

4 teaspoons baking powder

2 teaspoons cinnamon

1 teaspoon baking soda

1 teaspoon salt

1 cup blueberries

MAKES 24 MINI MUFFINS

1 Preheat oven to 375 degrees. In a large bowl, mix the bananas, yogurt, honey, oil, and vanilla.

2 In a medium bowl, mix all the dry ingredients together. Add the wet ingredients to the dry ingredients, stirring until just barely mixed.

3 Fold in the blueberries gently.

4 Grease a mini muffin tin. Scoop the batter into the tin evenly. Bake for 8–9 minutes.

5 Remove the muffins from the oven, and allow them to cool 5 minutes before transferring them from the muffin tin to a wire rack. Store the leftovers in an airtight container in the refrigerator.

TIP:
Make an extra batch of muffins to store in the freezer for later enjoyment.

BANANA BREAD BITES

THESE MINI MUFFINS ARE EASY TO WHIP UP AND DON'T USE *ANY* SUGAR OR HONEY!
THE NATURAL SWEETNESS COMES PURELY FROM THE BANANAS. IF YOUR FAMILY ISN'T
USED TO A LOW-SUGAR DIET YET, THEN ADD TWO TABLESPOONS HONEY. MY BOYS
GOBBLED THEM UP, EVEN WITHOUT HONEY.

INGREDIENTS

1 cup old-fashioned oats

2 ripe bananas, mashed (about 1 cup)

1 teaspoon cinnamon

1/4 teaspoon nutmeg

1 egg, beaten

1 cup white or red quinoa, cooked

MAKES 18 MINI MUFFINS

1 Preheat oven to 350 degrees. Mix together the oats, banana, cinnamon, nutmeg, and egg.

2 Gently stir in the quinoa.

3 Spoon the batter into a mini muffin tin. Bake for 20–25 minutes.

4 Remove the bites from the oven, and allow them to cool 5 minutes before transferring them from the muffin tin to a wire rack. Store the leftovers in an airtight container in the refrigerator.

DID YOU KNOW?

Quinoa contains concentrated levels of the antioxidant flavonoids quercetin and kaempferol, which help guard against free radicals that damage the body's cells—even more so than so-called "superberries" like lignonberry and cranberry.

MINI SPINACH FLATBREADS

I LOVE THE SEASONING IN THESE FLATBREADS. WE TOPPED THEM WITH THE HUMMUS ON PAGE 43 AND SOME SHREDDED VEGETABLES. IT IS A DELICIOUS, SAVORY SNACK.

1 Place the carrots, spinach, and warm water in a blender. Mix until consistent throughout.

2 Add in the rest of the ingredients and continue to blend until the batter is smooth.

3 Grease hands with olive oil and roll the batter into 1-inch balls. Put the balls in a bowl, cover with a dish towel or paper towel, and let sit 10 minutes.

4 Heat a skillet to medium heat.

5 Pass each ball back and forth between your hands to flatten.

6 One at a time, place the flatbread on the skillet and brown on both sides.

7 When cool, eat plain or with your favorite toppings. Serve immediately or store in an airtight container in the refrigerator.

INGREDIENTS

2 carrots, shredded

1 1/2 cups spinach

3/4 cup warm water

1/4 cup quinoa flour

6 tablespoons olive oil

3/4 teaspoon baking powder

1/2 teaspoon garlic powder

3/4 teaspoon salt

1 tablespoon basil

6 tablespoons cornstarch

Your favorite flatbread topping(s)

MAKES 6–8 FLATBREADS

PUMPKIN BREAD

PUMPKIN ANYTHING IS MOM'S FAVORITE FOOD ANY TIME OF THE YEAR. THIS PUMPKIN BREAD IS NO EXCEPTION, AND WITH JUST A HINT OF CHOCOLATE, YOU'LL HAVE A HARD TIME SAYING NO TO A SLICE.

1 Preheat oven to 350 degrees. Mix together dry ingredients in a medium bowl.

2 In a large bowl, mix together the remaining ingredients except the chocolate chips. Add the dry ingredients and then the chocolate chips, not stirring more than is necessary to combine.

3 Pour the batter into two small greased loaf pans. Bake for 25–30 minutes or until a knife inserted in the center comes out clean.

4 Let the bread cool for 5 minutes in the pan, then transfer to a wire rack.

INGREDIENTS

1 cup old-fashioned oats

1/4 teaspoon salt

1/2 teaspoon baking soda

1 teaspoon baking powder

1 cup quinoa, cooked

1/3 cup honey

1 egg

1 cup pumpkin puree

1/2 cup crushed chocolate chips

MAKES 2 SMALL LOAVES

DID YOU KNOW?

Pumpkin fanatics will be happy to know that in addition to being incredibly delicious, pumpkin actually has several health benefits, too! Pumpkin contains an extremely high percentage of vitamin A, which helps keep your eyesight sharp. Like quinoa, it's also high in fiber, helping you feel fuller for longer. It also can help lower cholesterol, reduce cancer risk, protect your skin, and improve your mood.

CHOCOLATE ZUCCHINI BREAD

THIS GLUTEN-FREE BREAD IS A HEALTHY WAY FOR US TO USE UP OUR ZUCCHINI WITHOUT ADDING A LOT OF SWEETENER.

INGREDIENTS

2/3 cup coconut oil

2 eggs

1 teaspoon vanilla

2 cups zucchini, grated

2 tablespoons cocoa powder

1 teaspoon baking powder

1/2 teaspoon baking soda

1 1/2 cups and 2 tablespoons quinoa flour

2 tablespoons cornstarch

MAKES 1 LOAF

1 Preheat oven to 350 degrees. In a large bowl, beat together the oil, eggs, vanilla, and zucchini. Set aside.

2 In a small bowl, whisk all the dry ingredients together.

3 Add the wet ingredients to the dry ingredients. Stir until just combined.

4 Pour the batter into a greased loaf pan. Bake for about 50 minutes or until a toothpick inserted in the center comes out clean.

5 Let the bread cool for 5 minutes, then remove from pan and transfer to a wire rack.

MUFFOOKIES

I HOPE THE NAME OF THESE TREATS PUTS A SMILE ON YOUR FACE LIKE IT DOES FOR US. MY SISTER SAID THEY WERE A COMBINATION OF A COOKIE AND A MUFFIN AND CAME UP WITH THE NAME. THEY HAVE SOME HIDDEN VEGGIES IN THEM, BUT THAT DIDN'T STOP MY DAD FROM SNEAKING A COUPLE BEFORE WE GOT A PICTURE OF THEM. MOM MANAGED TO SAVE A FEW FOR THE PHOTO—JUST IN TIME!

INGREDIENTS

1 1/2 cups quinoa flour

1/4 teaspoon salt

1 teaspoon cinnamon

1/2 teaspoon baking soda

3 tablespoons cornstarch

1/2 cup coconut oil

1/2 cup honey

1 egg

1 teaspoon vanilla

1 1/2 cups zucchini, grated

1/2 cup carrot, grated

2 cups old-fashioned oats

1 cup dark chocolate chips

1 Preheat oven to 350 degrees. In a large bowl, mix the flour, salt, cinnamon, baking soda, and cornstarch with a wire whisk until combined. Set aside.

2 In a separate bowl, beat together the oil, honey, egg, and vanilla until light and fluffy. Add the zucchini and carrots and blend until combined.

3 Stir the wet ingredients into the flour mixture.

4 Add the oats and then the chocolate chips. Let the mixture sit for a couple minutes to thicken.

5 Using a cookie scoop or two spoons, scoop the batter onto a cookie sheet lined with parchment paper or onto a greased cookie sheet.

6 Bake until light golden, about 10 minutes.

7 Cool on a wire rack and enjoy. Store leftovers in an airtight container.

MAKES 24 MUFFOOKIES

QUINOA TORTILLAS

WE ARE BIG FANS OF MAKING OUR OWN TORTILLAS. NOT ONLY ARE THEY DELICIOUS, BUT WHEN YOU MAKE THEM YOURSELF, YOU GUARANTEE THAT THEY ARE ONLY MADE WITH THE MOST BASIC, WHOLESOME INGREDIENTS.

1 Mix the ingredients together in a large bowl. Knead the dough by hand ten times, and then let it rest for 20 minutes.

2 Put cooking oil on your hands. Roll the dough into six balls. Pick up one ball and pass the dough back and forth between your hands to flatten it.

3 Heat a skillet to medium heat. Grease with nonstick spray or 2 tablespoons oil.

4 Place one flattened tortilla at a time in the hot skillet. Brown each side.

5 Add your favorite toppings. We enjoy the tortillas with beans, cheese, tomatoes, and cilantro.

INGREDIENTS

2 cups quinoa flour

1 teaspoon baking powder

1/4 teaspoon salt

1/4 cup coconut oil

1 cup water

3 tablespoons cornstarch

1/8 teaspoon chili powder

Your favorite tortilla toppings

MAKES 6
TORTILLAS

STRAWBERRY MUFFINS

WHO DOESN'T LOVE A STRAWBERRY MUFFIN? UNLIKE MOST MUFFINS, THESE ARE HEALTHY ENOUGH TO TRULY BE CALLED A NUTRITIOUS BREAKFAST. THEY WILL START YOUR DAY OFF RIGHT.

1 Preheat oven to 350 degrees. In a large bowl, mix together the dry ingredients.

2 In a second bowl, mix together the wet ingredients. Add wet ingredients to dry ingredients and mix until just incorporated—do not overmix.

3 Pour the batter into a greased mini muffin tin. Bake for 12–15 minutes. Let the muffins cool before removing them from the pan.

4 Enjoy the muffins, once cooled, and store leftovers in an airtight container.

INGREDIENTS

1 cup gluten-free flour

1/4 cup quinoa flour

1 teaspoon cinnamon (optional)

1/2 teaspoon baking soda

1/4 teaspoon salt

1 tablespoon cornstarch

1 egg

1/2 cup honey

2 tablespoons grapeseed oil

1 cup strawberry puree

MAKES 24 MINI MUFFINS

QUINOA BISCUITS

RATHER THAN ROLLING OUT AND CUTTING THESE BISCUITS BY HAND, WE MADE THEM IN A MUFFIN TIN. DOING SO SAVES PREP TIME FOR THIS QUICK AND YUMMY GLUTEN-FREE BISCUIT RECIPE.

INGREDIENTS

1 1/2 tablespoons cornstarch

1 3/4 cups quinoa flour

1 1/2 teaspoons salt

1 teaspoon baking soda

1/2 teaspoon baking powder

1 1/2 cups almond milk, unsweetened

2 tablespoons honey

2 eggs

6 tablespoons coconut oil

MAKES 12 BISCUITS

1 Preheat oven to 350 degrees. Mix dry ingredients in a medium bowl and set aside.

2 In a small bowl, beat the milk and honey. Continue beating, adding in one egg at a time and then the oil.

3 Make a well in the dry mixture and pour the liquid mixture into the hole. Stir until all ingredients are combined.

4 Scoop the batter into greased muffin pans or paper muffin cups. Bake for 10–12 minutes or until a knife inserted in the center comes out clean.

PIZZA CRUST

THIS CERTAINLY ISN'T YOUR USUAL FLUFFY PIZZA CRUST, BUT WE THINK YOU WILL LOVE IT ANYWAY. WHAT SETS IT APART IS THAT IT'S FILLING, HEALTHY, AND PERFECTLY SEASONED.

1 Preheat oven to 425 degrees. In a large bowl, beat the eggs with a fork. Mix in the garlic, baking powder, cheese, salt, basil, and olive oil.

2 Stir in the quinoa. Be careful not to make it too mushy, but mix the ingredients until completely incorporated.

3 Grease a cookie sheet or pizza pan. Pour the batter onto the pan and, with greased fingers, flatten the dough to 1/2-inch thick, making an 8-inch pizza.

4 Bake for 15 minutes, or until the crust begins to turn a golden color. Remove from the oven and add your favorite pizza toppings. Return the pizza to the oven and cook for 5 more minutes or until toppings are cooked.

5 Let the pizza cool for 5 minutes before serving. The cooling time will help keep the crust from crumbling.

INGREDIENTS

2 eggs

1 clove garlic, minced

1/2 teaspoon baking powder

2 tablespoons parmesan cheese, grated

1/4 teaspoon salt

1/2 teaspoon basil

1 tablespoon olive oil

1 cup quinoa, cooked

Your favorite pizza toppings

MAKES ONE 8-INCH PIZZA

97

ENTRÉES

QUINOA STACKS

THIS DISH IS A VEGETARIAN BURRITO WITHOUT THE TORTILLA. FULL OF PROTEIN AND FRESH VEGGIES, THIS IS AN EASY, FILLING MEAL TO PREPARE FOR OUR FAMILY.

INGREDIENTS

1 tablespoon olive oil

1/2 cup chopped onions

1/2 teaspoon cumin

1/4 teaspoon chili powder

1/4 teaspoon garlic powder

Salt and pepper to taste

2 cups quinoa, cooked

1 can (15 ounces) black beans, drained and rinsed

1 avocado, diced

1 cup cheese of your choice, grated

1/2 cup salsa

Lime juice

Cilantro

SERVES 4

1 Sauté the onions in oil until soft. Remove from heat.

2 In a small bowl, mix together the cumin, chili powder, garlic powder, salt, and pepper. Gently toss the spices into the quinoa, being careful not to make it mushy.

3 Place 1/2 cup quinoa on each serving plate. Divide beans among plates. Top with avocado, grated cheese, sautéed onions, and salsa. Garnish with lime juice and cilantro to taste.

THAI PINEAPPLE COCONUT QUINOA

A RECENT TRIP TO THAILAND INSPIRED THIS DISH. I WANTED TO RECREATE SOME OF THE AMAZING FLAVORS I EXPERIENCED THERE.

1 Set aside 1/4 cup of the coconut milk. Cook the quinoa in a large saucepan using the remainder of the coconut milk (about 1 3/4 cups) plus 1/4 cup water to equal 2 cups liquid. Bring the quinoa, coconut milk, and water just to a boil. Cover and reduce the heat to a low simmer for about 20 minutes. When all the liquid is gone, the quinoa is done. Place it in the refrigerator to cool. This will help prevent the quinoa from getting mushy.

2 In a small bowl, mix together the ginger, garlic sauce, lime juice, and reserved coconut milk. Set aside.

3 In a large wok or skillet on medium heat, add the grapeseed oil, green onions, cayenne peppers, bell pepper, and garlic. Toss until coated with oil. Sauté until the vegetables begin to soften. Add the shrimp and sauce, and continue cooking until the shrimp are warm.

4 Make a well in the middle of the vegetables and break the egg into it. Scramble the egg, and cook thoroughly. Mix in the quinoa and the pineapple, and let it warm up. Enjoy immediately, topped with pineapple.

DID YOU KNOW?

Though coconut milk has been somewhat infamous for its high saturated fat content, its fatty acids may actually aid weight loss, improve immune system health, reduce the risk of heart disease, and improve skin and hair. No need to feel guilty using it in your recipes!

INGREDIENTS

1 cup quinoa, uncooked and well rinsed

1 can (14 ounces) light coconut milk

1/4 cup water

1/2 teaspoon fresh ginger, grated

1 teaspoon chili garlic sauce

2 teaspoons lime juice

1 tablespoon grapeseed oil

3 green onions, diced

2 cayenne peppers, deseeded and diced

1/2 large orange bell pepper, chopped (about 1 cup)

2 cloves garlic, minced

12 large cooked shrimp, frozen

1 egg

1 1/2 cups fresh pineapple, chopped

SERVES 6

VEGAN QUINOA LETTUCE BURGERS

IN THIS RECIPE, WE USE FLAXSEED INSTEAD OF THE TRADITIONAL EGG TO BIND THE INGREDIENTS TOGETHER, MAKING IT VEGAN. SINCE QUINOA IS A COMPLETE PROTEIN AND FLAX HAS SO MANY OMEGA-3 FATTY ACIDS, THIS BURGER IS A GREAT MEAT SUBSTITUTE.

INGREDIENTS

1 1/2 cups quinoa, cooked

3/4 cup apple, shredded

2 green onions, chopped

1 tablespoon gluten-free Worcestershire sauce

1/2 teaspoon dry mustard

1/4 teaspoon salt

1/4 teaspoon pepper

2 cloves garlic

1/2 cup cornmeal

1 1/2 teaspoons flaxseed, ground

4 tablespoons water

Coconut oil

Tomato, sliced

Green leaf lettuce

MAKES 8 BURGERS

1 Mix together the quinoa, shredded apple, and green onions.

2 In a small bowl, mix together Worcestershire sauce, mustard, salt, pepper, and garlic. Pour over the quinoa and stir until combined. Stir in the cornmeal.

3 Using a blender, food processor, or electric mixer, beat together the flaxseed and water until the mixture becomes thick. Add to the quinoa and stir.

4 Heat a skillet to medium heat. Put a small amount of coconut oil in the skillet. Form a patty with your hands and place it in the pan. Brown on each side, taking care while flipping it over.

5 Place the patty on a paper towel to absorb extra oil. Let it sit for 5–10 minutes.

6 Top the patty with a thick tomato slice and wrap in several leaves of lettuce. Enjoy immediately.

DID YOU KNOW?

Flaxseed was cultivated by the Babylonians in 3000 BC. Scientists have been experimenting with flaxseed since the 1950s to better understand its health benefits, and evidence suggests that it may have an anti-cancer effect.

BARBECUE CHICKEN QUINOA SALAD

EVERYONE IN OUR FAMILY IS A BIG FAN OF BARBECUE SAUCE. MOM SAW A SALAD LIKE THIS ONE AT THE STORE, AND IT GOT HER THINKING ABOUT MAKING HER OWN VERSION. WE ADDED A LOT OF VEGETABLES AND QUINOA AND MADE A HEALTHIER DRESSING. THIS SALAD WOULD MAKE A GREAT BRUNCH OR DINNER. IT IS A NICE SUMMER MEAL OPTION, TOO.

INGREDIENTS

4 cups cabbage, chopped

2 cups spinach

1/2 cup carrots, chopped into bite-sized pieces

3–4 green onions, chopped

1/2 red pepper, sliced

1/2 orange pepper, sliced

1/2 yellow pepper, sliced

1/2 cup celery, chopped into bite-sixed pieces

1/2 cup cilantro, chopped

1 cup quinoa, uncooked and well rinsed

4 cups grilled chicken breast, chopped into bite-sized pieces

1 teaspoon salt

1/2 teaspoon pepper

1 cup plain yogurt

1/3 cup gluten-free barbecue sauce

2 avocados, sliced

Extra cilantro, chopped for garnish

1 Toss the greens, chopped vegetables, and cilantro together in a large bowl. Set aside.

2 In a medium saucepan, toast the quinoa for a few minutes on medium heat, stirring frequently, until it turns a light golden color. Let it cool, and reserve 2 tablespoons.

3 In a medium bowl, mix the quinoa, chicken, salt, pepper, yogurt, and barbecue sauce.

4 Toss the chicken mixture with the greens until incorporated.

5 Serve in the bowl or on individual plates. Garnish with avocado, cilantro, and the reserved toasted quinoa.

SERVES 8

DID YOU KNOW?

We wouldn't be here without—among other things—amino acids! When we eat high-protein food, such as quinoa, the acids in our stomach digest the protein and release amino acids that help build our tissues and organs. Think about that when you add the liquid aminos to the optional barbecue sauce recipe.

If you want barbecue sauce without all the additives, it is simple and easy to make your own. Just let the following recipe simmer while you are getting the rest of your meal ready.

BARBECUE SAUCE

3/4 cup tomato sauce
1/4 cup apple cider vinegar
1/2 cup brown sugar
1 tablespoon gluten-free Worcestershire sauce

1 tablespoon liquid aminos
1 1/2 teaspoons honey
1 tablespoon minced garlic
1/4 teaspoon ginger, ground

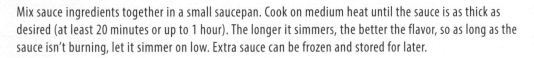

Mix sauce ingredients together in a small saucepan. Cook on medium heat until the sauce is as thick as desired (at least 20 minutes or up to 1 hour). The longer it simmers, the better the flavor, so as long as the sauce isn't burning, let it simmer on low. Extra sauce can be frozen and stored for later.

STIR-FRIED CHICKEN
AND CHINESE VEGETABLES

INGREDIENTS

....

2 cups water

1/4 cup barley, uncooked

1/4 cup quinoa, uncooked and well rinsed

1/2 cup brown rice, uncooked

2 cups chicken, cooked and chopped into bite-sized pieces

1/2 cup chicken broth*

1/4 tablespoon liquid aminos

1/2 tablespoon water

2 cloves garlic, minced

1 1/2 teaspoons fresh ginger, peeled and minced

1/2 teaspoon salt

2 teaspoons canola or coconut oil

3 cups bok choy, chopped

1 red bell pepper, deseeded and cut into 1-inch squares

1/2 small white onion, chopped

1/2 carrot, thinly sliced

1 cup snow or snap peas

1 can (8 ounces) sliced mushrooms

1/4 cup canned sliced water chestnuts, drained

Salt and pepper to taste

1 Boil water in a large pot. Add the barley, quinoa, and brown rice, and reduce the heat to a simmer. Cover and cook for 15–20 minutes. When the water is gone, remove the pot from heat. Set aside.

2 Combine the broth, liquid aminos, water, garlic, ginger, and salt in a small bowl.

3 In a large nonstick skillet, heat the oil. Sauté the bok choy, bell pepper, onion, and carrot slices for 3 minutes.

4 Add the broth mixture to the skillet along with the peas, mushrooms, and chicken. Reduce the heat and continue cooking, stirring frequently, for about 3 minutes. Add water chestnuts and cook for 1 minute longer or until they are heated through.

5 Add salt and pepper to taste, if needed. Add the vegetables and chicken to the grain mixture, and toss gently.

SERVES 4

TIP:

*For this recipe, Mom cooks her chicken on the stovetop in some water. When the chicken is done, the leftover water becomes her broth.

SPICY SHRIMP LETTUCE WRAPS

WE LOVE EATING SHRIMP, AND THEY ARE EASY TO INCORPORATE INTO MEALS OF MANY VARIATIONS. THESE WRAPS ARE DELICIOUS. THE ADDITION OF CHILI SAUCE ADDS A NICE LITTLE BITE TO THIS DISH.

1 Put the chopped shrimp in a large bowl. Add the rest of the ingredients except the lettuce leaves and quinoa.

2 Stir until combined. Do not overstir.

3 Scoop a spoonful of the shrimp mixture and a spoonful of quinoa onto each lettuce leaf, and enjoy.

INGREDIENTS

1 cup shrimp, cooked, peeled, deveined, de-tailed, and chopped

1 tablespoon fresh lime juice

1/4 cup cilantro, chopped

2 tablespoons fresh mint leaves, chopped

4 green onions, thinly sliced

3 tablespoons fish sauce

1/2 teaspoon salt

1 tablespoon chili garlic sauce

1 tablespoon peanut oil

1/4 onion, chopped

4–6 large romaine leaves, washed

1 cup quinoa, cooked

MAKES 4–6 WRAPS

QUINOA "FRIED RICE"

THIS DISH IS A TWIST ON THE OLD CLASSIC, USING QUINOA INSTEAD OF RICE. OUR VERSION CONTAINS LOTS OF VEGGIES TO MAKE IT EVEN HEALTHIER. ADD CHICKEN FOR EXTRA FLAVOR.

INGREDIENTS

2 cups water

1 cup quinoa, uncooked and well rinsed

1 tablespoon olive oil

2 cloves garlic, minced

1 tablespoon fresh ginger, minced

3 green onions, diced

1/2 red bell pepper, chopped

1 carrot, shredded

8–10 broccoli florets, chopped

3 tablespoons liquid aminos

2 eggs

SERVES 3

1 In a medium pot, bring 2 cups of water to a boil. Add the quinoa and cover. Boil 12–15 minutes until the water has evaporated and the quinoa is cooked.

2 In a large saucepan over medium-high heat, stir the olive oil, garlic, and ginger until fragrant, about 1 minute. Add the remaining vegetables and sauté for 3–4 minutes, until just tender.

3 Add the liquid aminos. Then add the quinoa and stir until just incorporated. Don't overstir or the quinoa will become mushy.

4 Make a well in the middle of the quinoa, and crack two eggs into the opening. Beat with a fork, and then allow the eggs to cook, attempting to not move the quinoa much during the process. When the eggs are cooked through, mix them gently into the quinoa. Serve immediately.

DID YOU KNOW?

The Food and Agricultural Organization (FAO) of the United Nations officially declared 2013 as "The International Year of Quinoa" because quinoa's biodiversity has made it instrumental in worldwide food security.

ROASTED RED PEPPER WRAPS

IF YOU PACK YOUR OWN LUNCHES, THESE WRAPS WOULD BE A GREAT CHANGE FROM THE USUAL SANDWICH. WE SUGGEST ROASTING YOUR OWN PEPPERS IT ALLOWS YOU TO ENJOY THE FULLNESS OF THEIR FLAVOR, AND IT'S EASY TO DO!

1 Preheat oven to 500 degrees. Line a cookie sheet with tinfoil. Place the pepper halves skin-side up on the cookie sheet. Cook for 20 minutes or until the skin is charred.

2 Remove the peppers from the cookie sheet and place in a zipper-sealed bag, or place in a bowl and cover with plastic wrap. Let the peppers steam in the bag or bowl for 10 minutes.

3 Remove the peppers and peel off the skin. It should peel easily after steaming.

4 In a small bowl, mix together the Greek yogurt, parsley, pepper, and garlic. Spread the mixture onto the tortillas.

5 Slice the roasted peppers into small strips and put on tortillas. Spoon half of the quinoa onto each tortilla. Roll the tortillas and serve. These wraps can be pre-made and refrigerated for an easy, packable lunch.

INGREDIENTS

1 red bell pepper, halved and deseeded

1 yellow bell pepper, halved and deseeded

1/4 cup plain Greek yogurt

1 tablespoon fresh parsley, chopped

1/4 teaspoon pepper

1/2 clove garlic, minced

2 gluten-free tortillas

1/2 cup quinoa, cooked

MAKES 2 WRAPS

TILAPIA TACOS

THESE TACOS ARE A DELICIOUS MEAL THAT WHIPS UP FAST. WE LOVE THE CREAMY SAUCE, AND YOGURT MAKES A GREAT SUBSTITUTE FOR SOUR CREAM.

INGREDIENTS

2 tablespoons olive oil

2 tilapia fillets, raw

1 cup plain yogurt

1 tablespoon fresh lime juice

1/4 teaspoon salt

12 corn tortillas

1 cup red quinoa, cooked

1 tomato, diced

1/2 cup cabbage, thinly sliced

Lime wedges for garnish

MAKES 12 TACOS

1 Heat oil in a skillet. Cook the tilapia in the heated oil for 3 minutes on each side until light golden. Take the fish out of the pan and place it on a plate lined with a paper towel to drain excess oil.

2 In a separate bowl, mix yogurt, lime, and salt together.

3 On each corn tortilla, place an even portion of fish and quinoa, top with yogurt sauce, and then add diced tomato and cabbage. Serve with lime wedges.

SALMON LOAF

SALMON LOAF WAS SOMETHING THAT MOM FREQUENTLY HAD AS A CHILD. IT WAS FUN TO CHANGE UP THE RECIPE BY ADDING QUINOA TO THIS DELICIOUS DINNER FOR ADDITIONAL HEALTH BENEFITS.

1 Preheat oven to 350 degrees. In a medium bowl, stir together all ingredients until incorporated. Grease a 2.5x5-inch loaf pan.

2 Gently press the mixture into the loaf pan. Bake for 25 minutes or until a knife inserted in the center comes out clean.

3 Let the salmon loaf sit for 10 minutes before slicing. Serve warm.

DID YOU KNOW?

Eating fish such as salmon that are high in omega-3 fatty acids has been shown to decrease risk of heart attack or stroke, high blood pressure, and high triglycerides. Experts say you can receive such benefits by eating just one serving of fish that is high in omega-3 fatty acids each week.

INGREDIENTS

1 can (14.75 ounces) salmon, drained

1 egg

2/3 cup quinoa, cooked

1/2 teaspoon garlic powder

1 teaspoon fresh lemon juice

SERVES 4

QUINOA ENCHILADAS

YOU'VE PROBABLY NEVER HAD ENCHILADAS QUITE LIKE THESE, SO GET READY TO BE PLEASANTLY SURPRISED. THIS IS ONE OF MY FAVORITE RECIPES IN THE BOOK!

INGREDIENTS

12 corn tortillas

2 cups black beans, cooked

1 can (28 ounces) green enchilada sauce

1/2 cup cheese

1 cup red quinoa, cooked

1 tomato, diced

Cilantro, for garnish

1 Preheat oven to 350 degrees. Grease a 9x9-inch square pan.

2 Layer the ingredients in the pan. First, add four tortillas torn up into 2- or 3-inch pieces. Then add 1/3 of the enchilada sauce, 1/2 of the beans, 1/2 of the quinoa, and 1/3 of the cheese. Repeat.

3 Add a final layer of tortilla pieces, enchilada sauce, and cheese. Then bake for 25 minutes.

4 Serve warm, topped with diced tomatoes and cilantro.

CHICKEN SALAD

CHICKEN SALAD IS A FAVORITE COMFORT FOOD, BUT IT DOESN'T SEEM VERY HEALTHY. THIS NUTRITIOUS REVAMP IS A CROWD-PLEASER.

1 Using paper towels, pat the chicken dry. Set aside.

2 Mix the quinoa, yogurt, and spices in a large bowl. Toss in the other ingredients, including the chicken. Mix until incorporated.

3 Serve the chicken salad on gluten-free rolls or tortillas.

INGREDIENTS

1 can (12.5 ounces) chicken breast, drained

1/2 cup quinoa, cooked

1/3 cup plain Greek yogurt

1/2 teaspoon garlic powder

Dash of pepper

1/4 teaspoon salt

1/2 cup celery, chopped

1/2 cup apples, chopped

3 green onions, chopped

SERVES 6

DESSERTS

MANGO QUINOA BROWNIES

THESE BROWNIES ARE MOIST AND DELICIOUS, THANKS TO MANGO—OUR SECRET INGREDIENT AND SUBSTITUTE FOR OIL AND BUTTER. THE MANGO ADDS MOISTURE WHILE KEEPING FAT LOW. AS ANOTHER HEALTH BENEFIT, WE ALSO INCLUDE VEGAN INGREDIENT ALTERNATIVES FOR THIS RECIPE.

INGREDIENTS

1 1/2 cups quinoa flour

1/2 cup oat flour

1 1/4 teaspoons baking powder

3 tablespoons cocoa powder

1/2 cup vanilla almond milk, unsweetened

3/4 cup mango, chopped

1/3 cup honey (vegan substitute: 7–8 softened dates)

3 tablespoons grapeseed oil

1 egg (vegan substitute: 2 tablespoons flaxseed, ground)

1/2 cup dark chocolate chips

MAKES 9 BROWNIES

1 Preheat oven to 350 degrees.

2 Stir the quinoa flour, oat flour, baking powder, and cocoa powder in a bowl until well combined. Set the bowl aside.

3 In a blender, mix the almond milk and chopped mango until smooth. Then add the honey, oil, and egg and blend until combined. Add the dry ingredients to the blender and mix until just combined.

4 Fold in the chips. Pour the batter into a greased 9x9-inch square pan and bake about 25–30 minutes or until the brownies pop back up when you press on them gently. Let the brownies cool, cut them into squares, and serve.

TIP:

We love to use stoneware dishes. They seem to cook baked goods, especially whole-grain baked goods, more evenly.

DID YOU KNOW?

There are numerous natural sweetener substitutes for sugar and the highly refined sweeteners that many of us use. In addition to mango, some examples—depending on the recipe—are: applesauce, mashed ripe banana, pureed dates, raisins or prunes, maple syrup, and fruit juice concentrate.

CHOCOLATE APPLE CUPCAKES WITH ALMOND BUTTER FILLING

WE HIT THE JACKPOT WITH THIS RECIPE! THESE CUPCAKES ARE HEALTHY ENOUGH TO HAVE FOR BREAKFAST BUT ARE ALSO A DELICIOUS DESSERT.

1 Preheat oven to 350 degrees. In a medium bowl, pour in the flour, cocoa, baking powder, baking soda, cinnamon, and salt. Stir with a wire whisk until all ingredients are combined.

2 In a separate bowl, whisk the oil, honey, yogurt, milk, and water for a couple of minutes.

3 Make a well in the dry ingredients and pour in the liquid mixture. Stir until just combined.

4 Fold in the grated apple until evenly combined.

5 Place cupcake liners in a muffin pan. Distribute the batter evenly among the cups.

6 Bake about 18 minutes or until a toothpick inserted in the center comes out clean. Cool on a wire rack.

7 To make the cupcake filling (ingredients on the following page) stir the almond butter, honey, and vanilla in a small bowl until smooth.

8 Sift powdered sugar over the cupcakes.

INGREDIENTS

CUPCAKES

1 3/4 cups gluten-free flour

1/4 cup quinoa flour

1/4 cup cocoa powder

2 teaspoons baking powder

1 teaspoon baking soda

1 teaspoon cinnamon

1/4 teaspoon sea salt

1/4 cup grapeseed oil

1/2 cup honey

2 tablespoons plain Greek yogurt

3/4 cup almond milk, unsweetened

1/4 cup water

1 apple, grated

FILLING

1 cup almond butter

2 tablespoons honey

1 teaspoon vanilla

DECORATION
SUPPLIES

Cupcake liners

Powdered sugar

Paper heart

Plastic sandwich bag

**MAKES 12
CUPCAKES**

9 Place a small paper heart on top of each cupcake and cut around it into the cupcake as deep as you want the filling to go. We cut about 1 inch down.

10 Scoop the filling into a plastic sandwich bag. Seal shut, releasing the air first. Cut a small piece off one corner of the bag.

11 Squeeze the filling into each heart cutout. You can use a butter knife to smooth over the tops. I dip my finger in a little water to level the tops for a perfectly smooth finish. Serve the cupcakes immediately; because they are so moist, the powdered sugar will absorb into them quickly.

TIP:

If you don't want to go to so much effort to decorate, follow these steps for each cupcake, and they will be just as cute: Frost the entire top using the almond butter filling as icing, then center a paper template of a heart on top, dust powdered sugar over the remaining surface, and remove the paper.

PERSONAL FRUIT PIZZAS

THE "SUGAR" COOKIES IN THESE PIZZAS LOOK PERFECT, ARE GLUTEN-FREE AND ENTIRELY WHOLE GRAIN, AND TASTE AMAZING—EVEN WITHOUT SUGAR. AS WITH MANY OF OUR RECIPES, THESE COOKIES AREN'T AS SWEET AS YOUR TYPICAL SUGAR COOKIE, BUT WE PREFER THAT AND THINK THEY ARE JUST SWEET ENOUGH.

1 Cream together the honey and coconut oil. Add the eggs and vanilla and mix until just combined.

2 Mix in the dry ingredients, adding the flour in small amounts until the dough is no longer sticky to the touch.

3 Place the dough in the refrigerator until chilled, about 1 hour.

4 Preheat oven to 375 degrees. Line a cookie sheet with parchment paper. Roll out the dough to be about 1/4 inch thick. Cut out the cookies into 3-inch hearts with a cookie cutter.

5 Bake for 7–8 minutes. Let cool on a wire rack.

6 Mix together the yogurt, honey, and vanilla in a small bowl. When you are ready to serve the pizzas, spread the yogurt mixture over the cookies and top with fruit.

INGREDIENTS

COOKIES

1 cup honey

2/3 cup coconut oil

2 eggs

1 teaspoon vanilla

2 cups brown rice flour

1 cup quinoa flour

1 teaspoon baking soda

TOPPING

2 cups plain Greek yogurt

1/4 cup honey

1 tablespoon vanilla

Fruit of your choice

MAKES 24 COOKIES

ALMOND BUTTER QUINOA BARS

MOM ENJOYS PEANUT BUTTER BARS, BUT SHE WANTED TO MAKE A HEALTHIER VERSION. AS MY SON RECENTLY SAID, "GRANDMA HAS HEALTHY TREATS!" AND HEALTHY TREATS CAN ALSO TASTE DELICIOUS.

INGREDIENTS

1 1/2 cups quinoa flour

1 teaspoon baking powder

1 cup almond butter

1/2–2/3 cup honey (depending on how sweet you want the bars to be)

2 eggs

1 teaspoon vanilla

Dark chocolate chips, shredded coconut, or dried fruit (optional)

MAKES 16 SMALL BARS

1 Preheat oven to 350 degrees. Stir the flour and baking powder together in a medium bowl.

2 Combine all the wet ingredients in a mixing bowl. Then stir the wet ingredients into the dry ingredients. Fold in the chocolate chips, shredded coconut, or dried fruit, if desired.

3 Pour into a 9x9-inch square greased pan (ceramic, if possible). Bake about 20 minutes or until a knife inserted in the center comes out clean.

4 Cool on a wire rack prior to cutting for easier and cleaner cuts.

QUINOA PUDDING

WE THINK THIS DESSERT IS A FANTASTIC SUBSTITUTE FOR YOUR FAVORITE OLD-FASHIONED RICE PUDDING.

1 In a small bowl, beat together 2 tablespoons of the almond milk and the egg yolk. Set aside.

2 In a large saucepan, combine the remaining almond milk, coconut milk, and butter. Heat the mixture on medium until it begins to steam. Then reduce heat to low.

3 Stir the quinoa into the heated milk mixture. Let the quinoa cook to your desired texture, stirring frequently to prevent burning.

4 Stir in the honey, salt, and egg yolk mixture until fully incorporated. Remove from heat and stir in the vanilla and cinnamon.

5 Cool to room temperature. Spoon the pudding into a large bowl or individual serving dishes. Cover with plastic wrap and refrigerate until completely cooled, then serve.

INGREDIENTS

2 tablespoons almond milk, unsweetened

1 egg yolk

2 3/4 cups almond milk, unsweetened

1 cup coconut milk

1 tablespoon butter

1/3 cup quinoa, uncooked and well rinsed

4 tablespoons honey

1/4 teaspoon salt

1/8 teaspoon vanilla

1/4 teaspoon cinnamon

Fruit for topping (optional)

SERVES 4

DID YOU KNOW?

Quinoa is technically a seed—not a grain. What criteria do you have to fulfill to be a grain? You have to be a seed of the grass family. That's why barley, wheat, and oats are grains and quinoa is not. Quinoa is more closely related to beetroots, spinach, and tumbleweeds!

LEMON CREAM CRUMBLE WITH STRAWBERRIES

MOM LOVES LEMONS. PAIR THEM WITH STRAWBERRIES, AND YOU HAVE A WINNING RECIPE IN OUR BOOK. THIS DESSERT TASTES LIKE LEMON CHEESECAKE AFTER IT'S BEEN REFRIGERATED.

INGREDIENTS

1 cup quinoa, uncooked and well rinsed

1/2 cup buckwheat groats, raw

1/2 cup raw, unsalted cashews, chopped

3 tablespoons coconut oil

2 tablespoons honey

1/8 teaspoon salt

1 cup plain yogurt

1 tablespoon honey

1 teaspoon vanilla

1 cup lemon curd

1 1/2 cups strawberries, chopped

1 In a medium saucepan, toast the quinoa for a few minutes on medium heat, stirring frequently, until it turns a light golden color.

2 In a blender, pulse the quinoa, buckwheat, and cashews until broken down into a crumble consistency.

3 Pour the mixture into a medium bowl and cut in the oil, 2 tablespoons honey, and salt with a pastry blender or whisk. Continue until well combined. If you want the topping to have more crunch, bake the mixture on a cookie sheet for 10 minutes at 350 degrees, stirring once.

4 In a small bowl, mix together the yogurt, 1 tablespoon honey, and vanilla. Set aside.

5 Fill four individual parfait dishes with about 1 1/2 tablespoons of the dry mixture in each dish.

6 Spoon 2 tablespoons yogurt mixture, then 2 tablespoons lemon curd, then strawberries into each dish.

7 Repeat the dish-filling steps again. Refrigerate or serve immediately. Top the dishes off with the remaining crumble and strawberries just before serving.

MAKES 4 PARFAITS

GINGERBREAD SNICKERDOODLES

WE ENJOY THIS GREAT COOKIE FOR CHRISTMASTIME, OR ANYTIME!

1 In a bowl, mix all the dry ingredients (except cinnamon and sugar) until well blended.

2 In a separate large bowl, beat the butter, honey, and egg until creamy.

3 Add the molasses, vanilla, and lemon zest. Stir until well blended.

4 Add in the dry ingredients slowly until dough is smooth. Refrigerate the dough for 30 minutes.

5 Preheat oven to 375 degrees. Mix together the cinnamon and sugar in a small bowl. Roll the dough into 1-inch balls, then roll them in the cinnamon-sugar mixture. Place on a cookie sheet.

6 Bake for about 8–10 minutes. Take them out just before they look like they are done.

INGREDIENTS

2 cups oat flour

1 cup quinoa flour

3/4 teaspoon baking powder

1/2 teaspoon baking soda

1/8 teaspoon salt

1 teaspoon ginger

1 teaspoon pumpkin pie spice

4 tablespoons butter, unsalted

1/3 cup honey

1 egg

1/4 cup molasses

1 teaspoon vanilla

1 teaspoon lemon zest

2 teaspoons cinnamon

1/4 cup sugar

MAKES 16 COOKIES

CINNAMON APPLE CAKE

WE DEVELOPED THIS RECIPE FROM AN OLD OATMEAL CAKE RECIPE. THE OATS AND QUINOA BALANCE EACH OTHER PERFECTLY AND LEAVE YOU WITH A NUTRITIOUS ALTERNATIVE TO BIRTHDAY CAKE.

INGREDIENTS

- 1 1/2 cups water
- 1 cup old-fashioned oats
- 1/3 cup coconut oil
- 2/3 cup honey
- 2 eggs
- 1 1/4 cups quinoa flour
- 2 cups quinoa, cooked
- 1/4 teaspoon salt
- 1 teaspoon vanilla
- 1 teaspoon baking soda
- 1/2 teaspoon baking powder
- 1/2 teaspoon cinnamon
- 1/2 cup shredded coconut, unsweetened
- 1 small apple, finely grated

SERVES 9

1 Preheat oven to 325 degrees. In a saucepan, boil the water. Remove the pan from heat, pour in the oats, and let sit for 15 minutes.

2 Cream the oil, honey, and eggs with an electric mixer. Then add the oats, flour, quinoa, salt, vanilla, baking soda, baking powder, cinnamon, coconut, and apple. Don't overmix.

3 Pour the mixture into a greased 8x8-inch square pan. Bake for 20–25 minutes or until a knife inserted in the center comes out clean. Serve warm or let cool.

BAKED PEACH COBBLER WEDGES

THE BEST PART OF COBBLER IS ALWAYS THE CRUST, SO IN THIS RECIPE, WE TAKE ADVANTAGE OF IT BY COATING RIPE PEACH WEDGES WITH DELICIOUS WHOLE-GRAIN TOPPING. SERVE THE COBBLER WITH ICE CREAM, MAKE IT FOR AN AFTER-SCHOOL SNACK, OR ENJOY IT TOPPED WITH COCONUT-FLAVORED GREEK YOGURT.

1. Preheat oven to 350 degrees. Beat the eggs and milk together in a small bowl. Set aside.

2. Put the dry ingredients into a blender or food processor and mix until the consistency is small crumbs. Put in a small bowl.

3. Dip the peach wedges into the egg mixture, then roll them in the crumb mixture. Place on a cookie sheet lined with tinfoil.

4. Bake for about 30–35 minutes or until fork tender— not mushy. Serve warm.

INGREDIENTS

1 large egg, beaten

1 tablespoon almond milk, unsweetened

3 tablespoons coconut sugar or brown sugar

1/2 cup old-fashioned oats

1/4 cup quinoa, uncooked, well rinsed, and dried

1/2 teaspoon cinnamon

1/4 teaspoon ginger, ground

Pinch of nutmeg

Pinch of cloves

1/4 cup raw, unsalted cashews, chopped

2–3 firm, ripe peaches, peeled and sliced into 1-inch thick wedges

SERVES 6

Volume Measurements

U.S.	METRIC
1 teaspoon	5 milliliters
1 tablespoon	15 milliliters
1/4 cup	60 milliliters
1/3 cup	75 milliliters
1/2 cup	125 milliliters
2/3 cup	150 milliliters
3/4 cup	175 milliliters
1 cup	250 milliliters

Weight Measurements

U.S.	METRIC
1/2 ounce	15 grams
1 ounce	30 grams
3 ounces	90 grams
4 ounces	115 grams
8 ounces	225 grams
12 ounces	350 grams
1 pound	450 grams
2 1/4 pounds	1 kilogram

Temperature Conversion

FAHRENHEIT	CELSIUS
250	120
300	150
325	160
350	180
375	190
400	200
425	220
450	230

ABOUT FAMILIUS

Welcome to a place where mothers and fathers are celebrated, not belittled. Where values are at the core of happy family life. Where boo boos are still kissed, cake beaters are still licked, and mistakes are still okay. Welcome to a place where books—and family—are beautiful. Familius: a book publisher dedicated to helping families be happy.

VISIT OUR WEBSITE: WWW.FAMILIUS.COM

Our website is a different kind of place. Get inspired, read articles, discover books, watch videos, connect with our family experts, download books and apps and audiobooks, and along the way, discover how values and happy family life go together.

JOIN OUR FAMILY

There are lots of ways to connect with us! Subscribe to our newsletters at www.familius.com to receive uplifting daily inspiration, essays from our Pater Familius, a free ebook every month, and the first word on special discounts and Familius news.

BECOME AN EXPERT

Familius authors and other established writers interested in helping families be happy are invited to join our family and contribute online content. If you have something important to say on the family, join our expert community by applying at:

www.familius.com/apply-to-become-a-familius-expert

GET BULK DISCOUNTS

If you feel a few friends and family might benefit from what you've read, let us know and we'll be happy to provide you with quantity discounts. Simply email us at specialorders@familius.com.

Website: www.familius.com
Facebook: www.facebook.com/paterfamilius
Twitter: @familiustalk, @paterfamilius1
Pinterest: www.pinterest.com/familius

THE MOST IMPORTANT WORK YOU EVER DO WILL
BE WITHIN THE WALLS OF YOUR OWN HOME.